A PORTFOLIO OF
KITCHEN
IDEAS

CONTENTS

© Copyright 1990, 1995
Cy DeCosse Incorporated
5900 Green Oak Drive
Minnetonka, Minnesota 55343
1-800-328-3895

Printed in Hong Kong

(0895)

Library of Congress
Cataloging-in-Publication Data
A Portfolio of Kitchen Ideas
p. cm.

ISBN 0-86573-970-6 (softcover)
1. Kitchens—Design and construction
I. Cy DeCosse Incorporated.
TX653.P65 1990
643'.16—dc20
90-33946

Author: Home How-to Institute™
Creative Director: William B. Jones
Project Director: Paul Currie
Project Managers: Carol Harvatin, Dianne Talmage
Writers: Carol Harvatin, Barb Machowski
Art Directors: Gina Seeling, Brad Springer
Copy Editor: Janice Cauley
V.P. of Development Planning & Production: Jim Bindas
Production Manager: Linda Halls

CY DECOSSE INCORPORATED

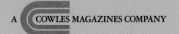

A COWLES MAGAZINES COMPANY

Chairman/CEO: Bruce Barnet
Chairman Emeritus: Cy DeCosse
President/COO: Nino Tarantino
Executive V.P./Editor-in-Chief: William B. Jones

A great kitchen is a culinary showplace offering easy care and convenience. A handsome, easy-to-clean butcher-block countertop helps the cook coordinate the activity in this busy country kitchen.

WHAT MAKES A GREAT KITCHEN?

A great kitchen is one created with your specific lifestyle in mind. It should be a comfortable, attractive and efficient place to work and socialize. Simply put, a great kitchen is a room your family loves.

To help you plan your great kitchen, we have assembled more than 150 color photographs of outstanding kitchen designs and features.

The first section of *A Portfolio of Kitchen Ideas* shows how you can customize your kitchen to reflect your family's lifestyle and tastes. It highlights the elements of a great kitchen: interesting color schemes, unique building materials, creative lighting, space-expanding storage units, and well-placed appliances and fixtures.

The second section has more than 50 pages filled with pictures of fantastic kitchens. Included are all the classic styles, ranging from traditional to country to contemporary. Also included are eclectic kitchens. This innovative style lets you step beyond the usual boundaries of design and decor to create your own personal look.

Whether you are sprucing up your old kitchen, planning a major overhaul, or designing a completely new kitchen, *A Portfolio of Kitchen Ideas* is sure to give you plenty of useful ideas.

Storage. *Pantry has adjustable wire baskets that will accommodate most containers. Swinging panels allow access to back shelves. For efficient storage, use vertical as well as horizontal space.*

Focal point. *Elegant brass range hood steals the show in this understated contemporary kitchen. Select one stunning feature, material or color, and make it the center of the kitchen plan.*

Color. *Buy a lot of style on a little budget. Accent a neutral scheme with bold, bright accessories, as in this white and red kitchen. A monochromatic color plan is soothing; high-contrast colors are lovely and energizing.*

PLANNING

Fit your lifestyle

Planning a kitchen starts with a close look at your family. How large is it? Is it growing? Consider your family's eating and cooking habits. Who eats at home? How often? Does your family eat together? Where?

Keep in mind the processes of food preparation, from baking bread to basting a bird. Consider how much cooking is done each week. Is there more than one cook? Are fresh or prepared foods more important? How often is equipment like a griddle, a food processor or pasta maker used? The answers to these questions will help you select appliances and estimate the food and equipment storage space that will be needed.

Include socializing in this lifestyle inventory. Does your family enjoy entertaining? How often? Where? For how many guests? Is entertaining informal or formal? Do guests help with kitchen duties? A floor plan begins to emerge as you consider how the kitchen relates to the entertaining areas.

Also list special family needs, such as space for a laundry, a sewing and ironing area, a phone center, a hobby counter or seating for children.

A large table is the center of activity for a busy family kitchen. Here, a large kitchen table becomes a colorful party table for a child's birthday celebration.

Bright white countertops *and flooring give this informal family kitchen a fresh, clean feel. For the family on the go, the convenient center island includes a cooktop with enough counter space around it to accommodate two diners.*

Photo courtesy of the National Kitchen & Bath Association

Create an exciting focal point in your kitchen. Put a ceramic-tile mural in the spotlight, for example, or pine cabinets stenciled with a country motif. Play up an architectural feature in an older home; create interest in a simple contemporary setting by using an unusual material for countertops or cabinets.

If you choose this bold approach to kitchen design, make sure the focal point is planned carefully in terms of scale, shape, color and materials. Visualize the kitchen as a complementary setting for the highlighted feature.

Focus on shape. *Lively angles define this unusual kitchen. The island and light fixture repeat the shape of the triangular room. The practical benefit: space is used efficiently.*

Photo courtesy of Armstrong World Industries, Inc.

Focus on a fireplace. *Floor-to-ceiling fireplace is the centerpiece of this contemporary kitchen. Details like a raised hearth, brick firebox, simple mantel and gleaming lamps enhance its appeal.*

Contemporary and country combine *in this clever kitchen design. The streamlined look of the cupboards and cabinets creates a smooth contemporary feel, while a country-style table with a butcher-block top is the centerpiece of this kitchen. The woven seats and old-style design of the chairs add a casual country accent that blends well with the contemporary design of the cabinets.*

By coordinating furnishings, accessories, colors and materials for any room, you can express your personal style. Usually this individual look reflects a classic style, such as stately traditional, casual country, sleek and simple contemporary or an eclectic mix of styles.

By studying the elements of classic styles in design books, store displays, design seminars and through consultations with kitchen planners, you can refine your planning skills. Careful planning is especially critical for those who are tackling a kitchen design project for the first time. Remember, function comes first in an active kitchen. Use simple treatments for cabinet fronts and countertops. Keep the flooring and window treatments simple as well.

Your goal is to create a kitchen that is a thing of beauty because it works so well, and also confidently expresses your personal style.

A classic black and white design scheme is created in a simple white kitchen by adding a striped awning and accenting with various black accessories. Clever choices of attractive accessories makes this kitchen fashionable as well as functional.

Distinctive double-arch cabinets dress up this cottage kitchen. Arched ceiling moldings repeat the cabinet pattern. Space expanding details; salmon and eggshell color scheme, drop-leaf rolling table stored under counter, and floor-to-ceiling cabinets.

Inspirational mix. Country/contemporary. Stark white kitchen is warmed with a wood ceiling, rustic antique dining table and American collectibles.

Photo courtesy of Merillat Industries

COLOR
Pulls a room together

A strong color scheme gives a kitchen character and unifies the design. Consider a monochromatic plan, in which one color, or shades of one color, dominates. Use this color on large areas, such as cabinets, counters or walls.

You can set a mood with color. Dark tones bring walls inward, creating intimate space; whites and neutrals open up a room. Warm up a north-facing kitchen with reds, yellows and oranges. Cool a warm-climate kitchen with white, blues and greens.

Warm peach walls glow under the recessed lighting. Oak cabinets take on a light wash of color from the warm walls. Soft green, a color complementary to peach, is a subtle accent.

Photo courtesy of Kitchens by Lynn

Pastels. Powdery blue-green furnishings set among neutral counters, walls and cabinets create a serene mood. The white ceiling and the wallcovering reflect light, adding a sunny, fresh feel to the room.

Bold and beautiful. *The colors in this painted stool coordinate with the printed fabric of the placemat and the small pictures on the wall, to bring a splash of color to this bright white kitchen.*

For dramatic visual impact, use splashes of bold color to accent a space. Intense hues, used judiciously, will enhance the contrast in a color scheme.

Lively accent colors are an effective way to prevent neutral color schemes from becoming too subdued. Areas of strong color can also be used to emphasize eye-catching details in a room that lacks architectural interest.

Bright yellow laminate counters accent this kitchen and dining area. Black and white in solids and patterns are an effective mix. Yellow dishes set on white tables create a vibrant contrast.

Deep, midnight blue countertops and walls are accented by brightly colored curtains in this traditional kitchen. The rich blue color creates a comfortable contrast to the warm tones in the cupboards, stools and woodwork around the room.

French blue knobs, *tambour doors, counter edges and molding give a country look to traditional raised-panel cabinets. Patterns make strong accents, too. Note the plaid wallcovering, bordered with blue molding.*

Photo courtesy of the National Kitchen & Bath Association

Skylights/spotlights. Two generous skylights allow the sun to flood the U-shaped kitchen. Spotlights on a track high in the vault provide general lighting. A second track brightens the cooktop area and turns a dramatic shine on counter and cabinets.

LIGHTING

Bright looks that really cook

An effective lighting plan combines general lighting with track lights and recessed ceiling fixtures. Task lighting, such as an under-cabinet fixture, is also important in kitchens for those times when you are working at the sink, cooktop or on the countertop.

Natural lighting is an important part of any kitchen plan as well. Skylights and openings high in the wall, such as clerestory or greenhouse windows, are superior sources of natural light.

Decorative accent lighting is taking a more prominent place in kitchen design. A popular choice: lighted glass-front cabinets.

Photo courtesy of WILSONART

Photo opposite page courtesy of Congoleum Corporation

Curved greenhouse windows span the work stations in an efficient galley kitchen. Cans mounted on a track (not visible) provide general lighting.

Multilevel lighting *is a must for efficiency in any kitchen. An overhead ceiling light, which provides general lighting, is combined with decorative task lighting over the island and recessed lights over the remaining countertops, to provide a full range of lighting options. The French patio doors also bring natural light into the kitchen during the daytime.*

A glass block wall makes a dramatic difference during the daytime in this contemporary kitchen. Natural light streams in to brighten the room and provide general illumination, while a pendant light above the table and a wall sconce provide additional lighting, when needed.

Eyeball fixtures, spaced to shine on the sink, cooktop and the walkway to the refrigerator, provide even lighting. Dramatic accent: glass blocks, lighted from inside the counter, shimmer with swirling patterns of icy light.

An adjustable lamp can be set at the proper height for those who prefer to be seated as they work. Pull the cord, and the lamp rises for those who like to stand while working.

LIGHTING

As you plan your lighting, try to bring in as much natural light as you can. If possible, try to plan windows on at least two different walls, or use another light source, such as a skylight, patio door or even a glass block wall, to balance the illumination from a single window.

Artificial light should provide both general illumination and task lighting. There are several approaches you can take to accomplish this. One way is to use recessed lights over all the counters and work areas. They focus light where it is needed and also throw off enough ambient light to provide general illumination.

Another approach is to use an overhead fixture, such as a pendant light, for general illumination. Then arrange task lighting where needed.

Accent lighting can be used to produce special effects. Spotlight or cabinet lighting can create stunning effects and dramatic moods.

MATERIALS

The building blocks of personal style

Simplify the process of selecting materials for your kitchen by shopping for one or two basics at a time. Tackle counters or cabinets first. Flooring and wallcovering may come next.

Cabinet shopping, for example, boils down to two basic choices: wood or laminate. Research cabinet styles, then select your material. Next, define the details, such as door style, finish or color, trim and storage components.

Flooring, wallcovering and counters offer a diverse range of choices. Some of the more contemporary materials include glass block, vinyl, marble, granite or hand-painted tile.

*A **custom-designed inlaid vinyl floor** achieves the elegant look of marble at the price of vinyl. Vinyl floors require minimal upkeep to stay looking great for a long time. And cooks will appreciate the softer surface vinyl provides underfoot for added comfort.*

Solid-surface material. *Man-made sheets, up to ¾ inch thick, rival the good looks of granite and marble. Sheets may be cut and shaped like wood. It is an expensive product, but it is durable and resists stains and burns.*

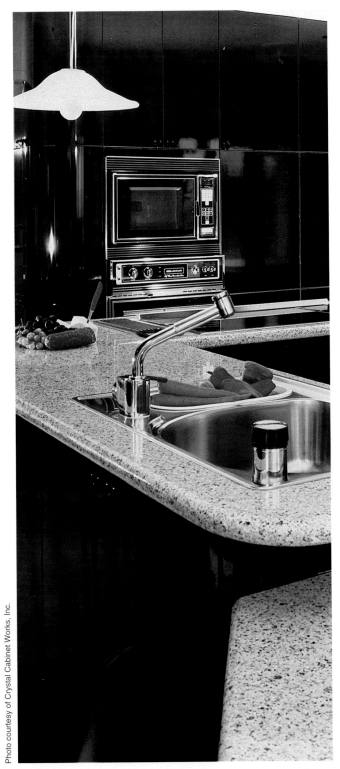

Laminates. *Flexible laminate sheets bonded to a substrate, usually particle board, make durable counters and cabinets. An array of dazzling colors and patterns is on the market. Above, dramatic high-gloss black laminate is bonded to curved cabinets.*

(right) **Ceramic tile surfaces** *create an eye-catching kitchen that's both functionally and aesthetically appealing. The natural color of the tile is an excellent complement to the olive green cabinets.*

Photo courtesy of Armstrong World Industries, Inc.

Photo courtesy of WILSONART

Glass block, *once a utilitarian material for basement and bathroom windows, now has a place in high-tech interiors. Glass block transmits light, creates stunning visual patterns and is suitable for structural uses such as the counter base shown above.*

Ceramic tile *laid in a bold geometric pattern borders an attractive island. Mix tile sizes and colors to create unusual, lively patterns.*

Photo courtesy of WILSONART

Photo courtesy of Interplan Design Corp.; photographed by DOMIN

Granite-textured laminate *is cut into strips and applied to a curved sliding door. Custom cabinets like this add eye-catching detail.*

Marble *is a great material for high-profile areas such as this wet bar. It will withstand a lot of wear and tear while maintaining its beauty.*

Ceramic tile. *Customize counters at a moderate cost with patterned tile, tile borders or designs created from tiles of different sizes and colors. Grout colored to match the tile is easier to clean than white grout. Above, earthy tile with floral insets creates a warm kitchen.*

Marble tile *in high-gloss black with a fine, white grain makes the island the centerpiece of this two-tone kitchen. Marble is a material that complements both traditional and contemporary decors.*

STORAGE IDEAS

Space-saving storage ideas

Storage systems in wood, metal or plastic are optional accessories in most cabinet lines. Select storage components that fit your budget and cooking style.

The following storage principles will help you organize your kitchen more efficiently.

Store items at the point of use. For example, locate pots and pans in drawers or on heavy-duty pull-out shelves near the cooktop. Fit storage to the items stored, such as divided cutlery trays for silverware.

If you want decorative appeal, try a colorful kitchenware display or hang shiny copper pots and pans overhead. Open storage visually enlarges a room, making it a wise choice for smaller kitchens.

Use every cubic inch of storage space. Don't waste space between shelves. A few of the excellent storage ideas available today are illustrated in the photos below and right.

Pull-out trays *store cleaning supplies, brushes and nonrefrigerated vegetables in sink base. Tilt-down sink panel turns wasted space into a storage area for pads, sponges and other supplies used at the sink.*

Linen trays. *Shallow sliding trays store linens without wrinkling the fabric. Ideal for tablecloths, placemats and cloth napkins.*

Swing-up shelf *is an ideal way to store less frequently used appliances, like this large mixer.*

Spice pantry and drawer. *Island storage puts spices and cooking ingredients within reach of the cooktop. Spice pantry is a fine example of sizing storage to the containers stored. The pull-out drawer allows full use of a deep cabinet.*

Roll-out serving cart glides out from under counter. The three-tier cart is hidden by a false cabinet door when stored. A space-saving accessory for entertaining.

Roll-out table is a big asset for small kitchens. It doubles as a counter or a table for two. Its lower work surface is ideal for pastry preparation. For storage, the hinged false drawer in the counter is lifted and the tabletop slides in; the table legs fit in recesses flanking the base cabinet.

Bread drawer, a fixture in kitchens in the days before preservatives, is lined with metal and ventilated to keep bread fresh. Pair a bread drawer with a cutting board to create a handy sandwich bar.

Corner cabinet trays rotate, bringing a collection of crockery into view. The wedge-shaped trays fit exactly on the shelves.

Photo courtesy of Wood-Mode Cabinetry

Photo courtesy of Wood-Mode Cabinetry

Photo courtesy of Crystal Cabinet Works, Inc.

Round cabinet/sliding doors. *Behind tambour-style doors are curved shelves for pots and pans, which are stored directly below the cooktop.*

Round cabinet/hinged doors. *Ultracontemporary island features curved laminate doors with European-style concealed hinges.*

Pull-out appliance drawer *frees valuable counter space. Full-extension slides ensure proper support for heavier appliances.*

Appliance garage. *Handsome trio of appliance garages with brass tambour doors saves on counter workspace. Two storage nooks hold coffee-making equipment, while a pull-out swivel shelf houses a portable TV.*

Multilevel storage. *Pantry with adjustable metal storage baskets is a cook's dream. Every can and package is visible. The tall storage racks in the lower section of the pantry rotate so the shelving behind is easily accessible.*

Pull-out pantry *fits neatly into a corner, flush with the laminate desk. Plastic-coated metal storage baskets hung on hooks provide flexible storage.*

Island pantry *is a wood variation of the multilevel storage system. Two door racks and the rotating racks inside have space-expanding adjustable shelves. A bonus: narrow shelves at the back of the cabinet are adjustable too.*

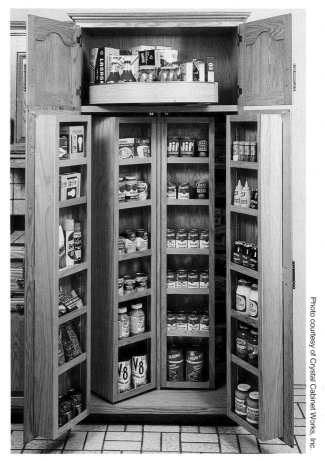

Pull-out table *topped with a cutting board is part of a complete baking center. In the upper cabinet are baking supplies, utensil racks, and a mixer plugged in and ready to use. Below the table, attractive wood drawers hold bake ware.*

Wood pantry, *which is more expensive than most basket storage systems, is a top choice for kitchens with fine wood cabinets. This pantry features a semicircular lazy susan in the upper cabinet, with adjustable shelves and rotating racks below.*

APPLIANCES & FIXTURES

Today's appliances offer features to fit every lifestyle. Cooktops with inserts for grills, griddles, deep fryers and rotisseries are available; refrigerator/freezers come in dozens of sizes and configurations; stainless steel, solid-surface and ceramic sinks now have one, two or three basins, along with numerous styles of faucets, sprayers and other attachments. And you can find ceramic and solid-surface materials in the latest colors. Down-sized appliances for small kitchens also are available.

A cleanup center is a top priority of almost every busy kitchen. Because up to 50% of your time in the kitchen is spent here, it's smart to pay special attention to sinks, faucets, and related items.

Cooktops add flexibility for special needs. Standard units come in gas or electric, and in finishes that include stainless steel, enameled cast iron or glass. Often you can interchange burners with a grill, a griddle or other specialty items.

Custom accessories turn an ordinary kitchen sink into a convenient work center. Cutting board insert, colander and mini drain board are just some of the options available.

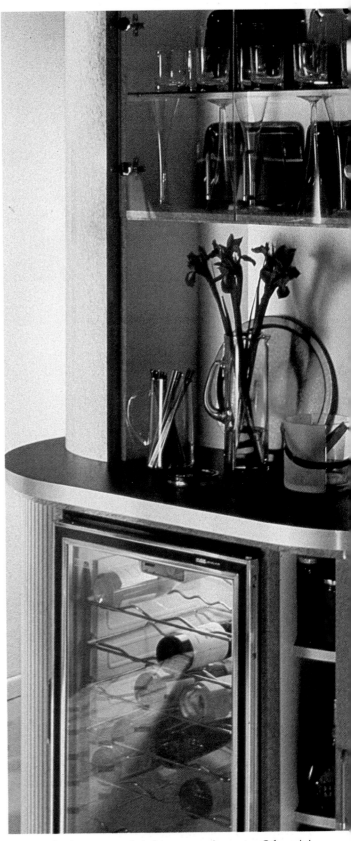

Wine cooler is a component of a beverage serving center. Other mini-refrigerators are designed for installation in island and base cabinets.

Gourmet island. A budding gourmet can take cooking lessons at this TV/VCR center. With the swiveling TV, the cook can follow recipe directions, in sequence, as he or she moves to work stations around the island. Details: black octagon sink, built-in wine rack, cookbook shelves, multiple storage drawers.

Corner sink *expands design possibilities for the small kitchen. The deep, single-bowl sink is located where it is most useful: between the dishwasher and the food preparation counter. An ideal fixture for a one-cook kitchen.*

Microwave/vent hood. *Multipurpose microwave has cooktop task lights and vents in its base. A low-profile vent hood for contemporary kitchens.*

(right) **Built-in refrigerator** *fits neatly into a custom cabinet with overhead storage. Bonus: wooden panels on refrigerator door match the rustic cabinetry.*

Commercial-style range *has four high-temperature gas burners, a griddle and a large oven. Textured range hood hides lights and powerful exhaust fans.*

A PORTFOLIO OF
KITCHEN
IDEAS

The fresh, contemporary colors and the country flavor are a winning combination in this contemporary country kitchen. The soothing colors provide the perfect background for the sleek Euro-style cabinets. Accents like shiny copper pots and pans and decorative bottles add a subtle country influence.

TRADITIONAL
Classically comfortable designs

A traditional room is inspired by the past and its time-honored decorations. From elegant and formal to simple and whimsical, the common thread throughout traditional design is comfort.

The cabinetwork sets the tone of a traditional kitchen. It is a showplace for finely crafted wood cabinetry. With many styles to choose from, the design may be simple and plain or detailed with elaborate moldings and panels. The type of wood used also influences the look of the finished cabinet. Oak, walnut and cherry are popular because of their distinctive grain.

Features like deep crown molding, roomy pantries, open shelving, appliances customized with wood front panels and glass cabinets are hallmarks of traditional styling. Accent with gleaming brass and copper accessories. You can also make a dramatic statement with colors and textures. Fabrics most often found in traditional kitchens are polished cottons patterned in florals, paisleys or stripes.

Classic design details were used in the moldings and raised wood paneling of the cupboards to give this kitchen a traditional mood. Sheer, flowing draperies on old-fashioned Palladian windows continue the traditional look in this kitchen.

Traditional design has many definitions: English traditional, French traditional, and the ever-popular American traditional, consisting of all-wood cabinetry finished with detailed molding and a vinyl floor. A small window above the sink is another popular detail found in traditional American kitchens.

To give one of these typically American kitchens a traditional English flavor, try changing the color of the floor to a deep crimson brick or rich orange terra-cotta tile. Paint the furniture a deep hunter green, then accent with rich red.

To achieve the flavor of a traditional French kitchen, pay attention to the small details. Use detailed French moldings on the cabinetry and paint to highlight the intricate detail. On the windows, use shutters that match those used on the cupboards.

Whether you decorate with 18th-century antiques or modern-day reproductions, traditional designs add warmth and comfort to a kitchen.

Distinctive double-arch cabinets dress up this cottage kitchen. Arched ceiling moldings repeat the cabinet pattern. Space-expanding details: salmon and eggshell color scheme, drop-leaf rolling table stored under counter, and floor-to-ceiling cabinets.

(below) *A traditional plaid* adds a decorative touch of color to this old-style serving tray.

TRADITIONAL

Today we appreciate the furniture and accessories of the past for features like solid design and attention to detail. A traditional kitchen has a sense of sentimentality that is expressed through collectibles like classical figures, bottled ships or family heirlooms. A traditional Victorian look can be achieved with the materials used in window treatments and wallpapers. Flowing draperies, shirred valances, shutters and swags are ways to give a window traditional dressing.

The way you accessorize a traditional kitchen adds to its overall richness. Bring life to a kitchen with lush ivy or flowers. Fill a traditional iron pot rack with polished copper pans, and hang a ceiling fixture of brass and glass.

Another necessary ingredient for classic kitchen design is practical storage space. In a traditional kitchen, this might include glass-fronted cupboards, which can also be used as attractive displays.

***Glass-front cabinets** with decorative mullions and brass accessories are accompanied by detailed woodwork to bring traditional style to the classic look of this kitchen.*

Select wood cabinetry for a warm contemporary look. Sleek European cabinets are available in a variety of hardwoods and stained finishes. Consider other uses of wood: on butcher-block counters, for cabinet trim and pulls, on light fixtures, around windows and doors.

Photo courtesy of Bruce Hardwood Floors

The cool, classic look of marble is incorporated into the countertops, providing a decorative yet durable surface for the island and countertops of this kitchen. The elegant look of marble is continued in the faux marble design of the vinyl floor. Plenty of counter space for food preparation and ample seating are provided.

Traditional with a twist. *The interesting and unusual shape of this center island follows the floor plan of this colorful kitchen; its generous size provides a place for storing pots and pans on one side and open shelves on another.*

TRADITIONAL

Islands that fit your lifestyle

Kitchens of the last century were dominated by a large, central work table. Today, the kitchen island replaces that old-fashioned table. An island expands counter space, increases storage capacity and provides an area for casual dining.

Drop in a cooktop with down-draft ventilation, plumb a second sink or wire an electric outlet in the island. For entertaining, invite guests to sit at the island while dinner is being prepared.

Rich turquoise accents outline pastel pink cabinets and add a dash of summer color, creating a warm, sunny kitchen. The cabinets were given a pickled finish that makes them appear weathered by the sun.

TRADITIONAL

The center island is the heart of many family kitchens. Often topped with butcher-block or marble, it provide surfaces for food preparation and serving. It often has built-in storage spaces or shelves to keep things close at hand.

A kitchen island is also a gathering place where friends sit and chat, as well as a casual eating counter for busy families that eat on the run.

Subtle textures and colors *add interest to the monochromatic composition of this kitchen. The straight, sleek lines of the cabinets in this classic kitchen give the room a contemporary twist. The clean, bright white cupboards are offset by the interesting texture of the walls.*

Entertain beautifully *in an elegant kitchen/dining area with matching cabinetry. Oak buffet contains bar sink, glass storage and wine rack for beverage service. Curved kitchen peninsula topped with granite-pattern laminate is convenient for serving and clearing the table. Soft gray wallcovering and flooring unite the area.*

A great floor plan maximizes the efficiency of the space. Some of the most common kitchen plans include: the U-shaped kitchen, three walls of work space; the L-shaped kitchen, a good plan for a small kitchen area; the corridor kitchen, with extra-wide aisles to accommodate through traffic; and the island kitchen, which adds an island to a U- shaped or L-shaped floor plan.

A spacious center island adds valuable counter space in this colorful kitchen. A classic checkerboard design gives the floor an old-fashioned appeal that is reflected in the seats of the tall bar stools. Fresh white cabinets and a shiny black and stainless steel oven add classic, yet contemporary, appeal.

COUNTRY

Charming Country Kitchens

Country means comfort, great food, good company. The country kitchen is a relaxed, informal room that combines modern convenience with easygoing charm. Define the style with naturals like pine cabinets, plank flooring, willow baskets and stoneware.

Fill your country haven with heirloom quilts and hand-carved furnishings or displays of collectibles. Country mixes well with almost any style, from Victorian to contemporary, so it's easy to modify the look of your country kitchen.

Photo courtesy of Armstrong World Industries, Inc.

Hefty beams and posts *set a country mood. Weathered cabinets with wrought-iron hinges conceal the refrigerator and provide storage. An antique woodstove shares kitchen duty with a modern cooktop. Overhead, a lively collection of baskets and cookware.*

Rustic furniture *incorporates authentic tree limbs for an eye-catching addition to this clever country kitchen. The weathered look of the color-washed cabinetry seems right at home next to a modern sink and faucet. Live plants, decorative baskets and copper cooking utensils add to the collective country look of this kitchen.*

Updated country kitchen *combines tile counters and rich oak cabinets with massive beams and vintage kitchenalia. Flavor the mix of old and new with whitewashed walls and a cooktop set into a curved alcove.*

COUNTRY

The friendly feel of a country kitchen is warm and comfortable. Filled with handcrafted furniture, natural textures and charming collectibles, country kitchens offer a sense of hospitality.

Country can also span many moods and varying styles. Spacious farmhouse kitchens have solid construction, stone, brick or tile floors and often a network of smaller storage rooms or pantries. The functional French country kitchen centers around food and its preparation, with shelves filled with spices and seasonings, and cooking utensils scattered about. American country brings to mind the image of large, rough ceiling beams, hand stenciling, stucco, glazed crockery, copper pots, linen and gingham and baking bread.

Photo courtesy of Wood-Mode Cabinetry

Photo courtesy of Dura Supreme

Hearty country cooking requires pots and pans in abundance. A handsome display of gleaming cookware hangs from butcher hooks on a sturdy pot rack above the island. Plate rack shows off Colonial-era pewter dishes.

The look of French country *has been captured in this charming kitchen. White enamel cabinets are the backdrop for this cheerful setting, which was created by adding blue and yellow patterned fabrics, fruit-embossed earthenware, and a baker's rack.*

Natural wood cabinets *feature porcelain knobs for a country emphasis. Advertising art, an egg basket, and other country pieces are set off by contrasting bright blue tiles.*

(photo left) **Painted detailing** *is an easy and inexpensive way to brighten a kitchen. The clever design of this country-style chair is just one idea that works.*

COUNTRY

Use natural materials. *Woods like pine, light oak and maple go with the country style. Antique maple butcher-block is an all-purpose workspace. Sturdy butcher-block counters are set on primitive cabinets. A wooden paddle fan blends with the pine ceiling.*

Photos this page courtesy of Kitchens & Baths by Design;
David Skomsvold, designer; Ed Cox, Michael Raabe, contractors

Fresh country. *It's always spring in this pastel-and-white kitchen. Flowers bloom on the contemporary-style wallcovering. A tile border of pale blue garlands accents the counters and walls. High-quality oak cabinets with brass pulls and a pair of rush-seat chairs embellished with flowers set a formal tone.*

Barnyard geese *wearing floral collars look right at home by the bay window. Large-scale accessories like these life-size animals enhance a theme kitchen.*

*The **whitewashed** look of the cabinets and cupboards gives this quaint country kitchen a farmhouse feel. An old-fashioned authenticity is created by the ribbed texture in the cupboard doors and drawer fronts.*

Country blue pinstriped wallpaper sets the backdrop for the rainbow of country colors in this kitchen. Apple green and sunny yellow are picked up in the dishes. Copper cookware and wooden ducks are some of the other country influences found here.

COUNTRY

Why not dine in your country kitchen, close to the aromas of good cooking? Basic ingredients: a generous table and wide, comfortable chairs. Keep the service informal, and add fresh or dried flowers to the table.

Underfoot, consider natural wood or flagstone topped with an old-fashioned rag rug. Overhead, exposed beams, barn boards or brick walls can be used to set a rustic backdrop. Or paint the walls a crisp white to add a contemporary look.

Checked backsplash *area has been sponge-painted with blue paint for a dramatic effect and a unique textured look. Checked walls add visual interest to the spaces above and below cabinets.*

COUNTRY

Classic patterns: plaids and small prints and fabrics with a hand-loomed look fit the casual criteria of country. Antique linens have a delicate heirloom appeal. Show off your favorite treasures by displaying collectibles around the kitchen. Other typical accents found in a country kitchen are whitewashed walls and pine furniture.

Checked gingham and small all-over print cottons are found in various spots throughout a country kitchen. Other features include stenciled borders and painted floors and floorboards.

Fresh-cut flowers, *captured in tile, decorate the range hood and wall. Bands of blue enhance the floral pastels. The textured hood surface resembles the whitewashed walls found in traditional French country homes.*

(below) **The home-style atmosphere** *in this kitchen is created by combining light woods with dark. A farm-style table and other practical furnishings bring a simple variety, while cluttered displays of cooking utensils are kept within easy reach.*

American country brings to mind the image of large, rough ceiling beams, hand stenciling, stucco, glazed crockery, copper pots, linen, gingham and baking bread.

American country style also includes designs with a southwestern flavor. They incorporate the patterns and colors used in the designs of American Indian clothing and artwork, and the natural colors found in the western desert.

The colors in a country kitchen are the colors seen just outside the window. They include sunny yellow and spring green. Country blues are sky blue or indigo "blue-jean" blue. Unnatural colors are blatantly out of place in a country kitchen.

(below) **Southwestern influence** *inspires the casual look of this country table setting.*

Photo courtesy of DuraSupreme

Country-modern *kitchen unites contemporary colors and classic cabinetry. Two-color laminate counters and a checkerboard floor dominate the room. Wallcovering and curtain fabric in small-scale patterns coordinate with the colorful accessories.*

(photo right) ***A decorative bracket*** *with a heart cutout, and decorative bottles are a few simple details that add to the country look of this country kitchen.*

Photo page 62 and this page courtesy of Cy DeCosse Inc.

Smooth laminate cabinets *and shiny chrome furniture set the contemporary tone in this kitchen. The laminate cabinets are a soft, two-tone beige that is repeated in the refrigerator as well. The faux marble design of the vinyl floor adds to the appeal of this sophisticated setting.*

CONTEMPORARY

Sleek and streamlined, a contemporary kitchen follows the design adage, "form follows function." Soothing curves, understated background colors and exciting textures combine to create a mood that's sophisticated, yet soft; worldly, yet warm.

A new chapter in kitchen design began when traditional cabinets were manufactured with light or natural finishes. Cabinet construction has been updated, too. Many styles are frameless, so doors and drawers fit flush; no cabinet frame is visible. The cabinetry blends beautifully with contemporary patterns and colors in wallcovering, flooring and window treatments.

The most efficient floor plan: an L-shaped kitchen with island. The refrigerator, sink and cooktop are within easy reach. The solid-surface counters and white ceramic tile island lighten the room. Wood panels camouflage the refrigerator and dishwasher.

Streamlined describes the clean, crisp contemporary look. The mix of materials and patterns for maximum effect. Sleek European-style cabinets with overlay doors are the top choice for this style. Sophisticated looks combine curving shapes, dramatic color schemes and high-gloss finishes. Color favorites: whites and neutrals.

Basic black polished-granite counters teamed with gray laminate cabinets create a dramatic two-color kitchen. Eye-catching angles: triangular dining counter complements cabinets rising across the wall.

(left) *Rich maple cabinetry* is detailed with contrasting trim and decorative brass hardware. The dramatic effect of the thick marble countertops is echoed in the elegant styling of the inlaid vinyl floor.

Photo courtesy of Interplan Design Corp.; photographed by DOMIN

Photo courtesy of Amtico Company Limited

Contemporary is sleek and sophisticated. Early modern design was pure white and uncluttered. Later, new shapes were made possible by new materials and new technology. Pieces were being made of glass and chrome, plexiglass or plastic. The influence of European modernism resulted in an International style.

Euro-style kitchens have clean lines and dramatic colors. You'll find frameless cabinets of high-gloss lacquer or laminate that house efficient storage units like lazy susans and wire frame pull-outs. Appliances are also built in, including the refrigerator and microwave.

(photo left) **Sleek Euro-style cabinetry,** *with sharp black accents, gives this contemporary kitchen a formal, finished feel. The rich wood tones add warmth and keep the room from looking dark and industrial.*

(photo left) **A soaring wall** *neatly frames the kitchen. Curved counter and simple stools invite guests to perch. An unusual use of pastels in a contemporary kitchen.*

Photo courtesy of WILSONART

Photo courtesy of Amtico Company Limited

Contemporary kitchens are free of clutter. Countertops and cabinets are bare and streamlined. Cabinets in modern kitchens are usually frameless, and often covered with laminate. Countertops generally consist of a solid-surface material, a slab stone like marble, or stainless steel—or they are finished with laminate.

Kitchens with a contemporary design are laid out to make limited space more efficient and usable. Windows have minimal treatments or are left untrimmed, and kitchen equipment is hidden out of sight to help maintain the uncluttered look.

The ultracontemporary design of the inlaid vinyl floor brings the look of the future to this Euro-style kitchen.

Contemporary neoclassic style *sets the mood in this monotone kitchen. Black marble countertops and black lacquer in the dining room furniture and barstools add a formal accent to the natural wood cabinetry.*

White: pure and simple provides a fresh, crisp look that is carried throughout the room. The materials that create the contemporary style are often in the form of ceramic tiles, laminate countertops and vinyl floor coverings.

In modern kitchens, the emphasis is on function. They are efficient and easy to maintain. Because many of the appliances are built in and compact, a contemporary design is a wise choice for a small kitchen.

(below) **Silverware holders** *beautifully accessorize any table. Depending on the materials used, they can have a simple tailored look or, with lace trim added, a more Victorian look, as shown here.*

Photo courtesy of Interplan Design Corp.; photographed by DOMIN

Focal point. *Gleaming copper and brass hood is the centerpiece of this kitchen, set off by white raised-panel cabinets, white counter and floor. Brass rails and cabinet pulls shine under recessed lights.*

Blue-gray trim *forms a horizontal pattern on simple white cabinets in this small kitchen. Shallow cabinets above the sink increase storage without projecting into the work area.*

This cozy little kitchen looks bigger and brighter with all-white cabinets and a white refrigerator. Primary colors are splashed throughout in the tablecloth and art work; even the appliances are bright and colorful. The sleek look of the solid material adds a contemporary feel to the decor and a sense of balance to the room.

(photo left) **A bold mix** *of rosewood and laminate creates a light, contemporary cabinet in spite of the dark stain. Rosewood crafted in the window frame, cabinet pulls, corner shelving and plank ceiling unify the design.*

Photos pages 76-77 courtesy of Wood-Mode Cabinetry

(photo above) **Contemporary curves** *dominate the wood-and-laminate storage wall and multilevel counter. Simple flooring and wallcovering form a neutral background for the high-contrast cabinet materials.*

CONTEMPORARY

Regional style. *Southwestern galley kitchen tucked behind adobe fireplace mixes sleek European cabinets with rustic counters. Regional elements: rough ceiling beams, carved stool and plank shelving lined with copper cookware, baskets and earthy pottery.*

(photo left) **Smooth lines** *of the European-style cabinetry give this kitchen a contemporary quality. Traditional accents like a pewter teapot on the stovetop are sprinkled throughout.*

Photo courtesy of Armstrong World Industries, Inc.

Photo courtesy of Congoleum Corporation

Circles and curves *dominate this gray and black kitchen. Multilevel island with vertical laminate is the focal point. Storage wall on the left and cabinetry on right were custom-made for the curved floor plan.*

Spice racks *recessed into wall below granite-patterned cabinets are close to the mixing area. Detail: sculpted recess in solid-surface panel holds fresh flowers.*

Shiny black lacquer countertops, *baseboards and trim beautifully contrast with the polished maple cabinetry. The delicate stripes in the high-style inlaid vinyl floor tie the two together in subtle sophistication.*

New Orleans-style *great room is summertime cool in crisp white and sky blue. Garden greenery, lazy fans and louvered shutters define the romantic Southern look. The spice: triangular island that centralizes cooktop, sink, dishwasher and storage.*

ECLECTIC

Classic kitchens with updated styling

The most exciting kitchens are a dynamic blend of classic and personal style. So go ahead and mix, whether your taste is traditional, country or contemporary. Find inspiration at home in a treasured antique, a bright poster, travel souvenirs or grandmother's floral china. Here are a number of stunning kitchens to get you started.

Traditional redefined. *Light, natural finish and European overlay doors update the traditional raised-panel cabinets. More contemporary touches: white and tan tile, whitewashed range hood, pearly solid-surface counters, soaring cathedral ceiling.*

Because kitchens usually have a great deal of woodwork, they offer the perfect opportunity to use popular new decorative paint finishes like color washing or a farmhouse finish. Farmhouse, pickled and crackled paint finishes are often used to give wood a worn, lived-in look.

To add color, cabinetry can be finished with the clean, bright look of enamel. Color-washed finishes are another way to add a subtle hint of color while still allowing the wood grain to show through.

Photos on pages 84-85 courtesy of Cy DeCosse Inc.

Hand-painted stool is the source of color for the subtle accents and accessories in this cheery kitchen. The high-gloss latex enamel provides a durable, smooth finish.

This eclectic kitchen incorporates contrasting styles of contemporary and country, with a sprinkling of Art Deco as well. Deep blue blankets the walls and countertops, unifying the entire room.

Create a unified look by embellishing table and chairs with wallcovering cutouts.

(opposite page) ***Pretty in peach.*** *Contemporary colors lighten and brighten this traditional kitchen. Classic frame-and-panel cabinets have the look of whitewashed wood. This same weathered look is found in the parquet wood floor as well.*

(right) ***Arched glass doors*** *extend above the cabinets to create a stunning look. Dark cabinet interiors set off white tableware on display.*

(below) ***Curved panel*** *joins sink cabinet and contemporary-style drawers. Art Deco designers experimented with new materials, like plastics. These high-gloss laminate cabinets and chrome-and-plastic drawer pulls are reminiscent of that tradition.*

Photos this page courtesy of WILSONART

Nothing renews the look of a room faster than strong colors, bold shapes. For a light, crisp look, paint everything white; then accessorize with colorful accents, such as colorful dishes or decoratively displayed cookware.

Vibrant colors as well as pastels can also be used to revive the look of a kitchen. Appliances available in new designer colors are another way of bringing color into a kitchen. Small accents like window treatments, lighting fixtures, cookware racks and colorful linens are little things that add personality and style.

Square power. *The simple square is given the spotlight in this black and white kitchen. Squares appear in the checkerboard flooring, white ceiling and black ceramic wall tiles.*

White alcove *is set off by black ceramic tiles with red grout. The gentle arch of the alcove contrasts with the squares that dominate the kitchen's design.*

The Art Deco design of the vinyl floor creates a dramatic backdrop for this cleverly decorated kitchen. The center island has a black high-gloss countertop that adds a sleek contemporary feel to the setting. Glass block added to one side of the island traps and reflects light for added interest.

Dynamic colors *unite three rooms in this open-plan home. Kitchen colors are balanced; no single hue dominates. Black appliances contrast with white cabinets and bright yellow counters. Distinctive details: textured black walls, mini-tables, Oriental-style chairs, sliding doors.*

Color communicates with us on physical and emotional levels and influences all elements in a room, from the furnishings to the fabrics. By taking advantage of the mood-setting qualities of color, you can design a kitchen that makes a personal statement.

Because color makes surfaces visually advance or recede, you can effectively use color to create visual illusions and transform the look of a room. Square up a long, narrow room by painting walls in advancing and receding colors. For example, a warm hue on a short end wall will bring it forward visually. A high ceiling can be lowered by using a color such as brown or blue to visually bring it down. Visually raise a ceiling with white or a light pastel.

Kitchens also need a balance of textures to keep the look harmonious. The slick, shiny surface of lacquer works best with other smooth surfaces, like stainless steel, ceramic and smooth marble; while rough, uneven textures, like brick or field stone, work best with textured surfaces, like wicker or unfinished woodwork.

Purely Oriental. *Traditional Japanese screens enclose an intimate dining area with mustard-colored walls. Lacquered dining table, red dishes and Oriental-style chairs enhance the Eastern theme. In the compact kitchen: black* shoji *screen, black cabinetry, black plate rack.*

Spacious kitchen blends turn-of-the-century charm with contemporary good looks. Old-fashioned details include painted cabinets, graceful hanging lamp, Palladian window and paneled ceiling. Brass range hood is set off by diamond-pattern wall tile.

Collector's kitchen mixes 19th and 20th century design. Crisp white European cabinets are topped with a display of Americana. Antique pine refectory table complements the country hutch displaying heirloom china. The butcher-block island counter, pine cathedral ceiling and bleached flooring warm the white walls and cabinetry.

Most people are at ease with a somewhat eclectic look. Mixing and matching makes this type of decorating exciting and allows you to stretch your imagination.

Decorating an eclectic kitchen is an art that is easy to acquire. Expressing your unique style requires defining your personal tastes, then slowly mixing the elements of different periods and styles to create just the right balance to reflect the real you.

Essentials. *Ultrasleek kitchen bares its walls and virtually eliminates decoration. The result: contours of the distinctive island and overhead light panel have a big impact. Sink, cooktop, storage and serving bar are housed in the long, curved island. Unusual focal point: stairway silhouette.*

Photo courtesy of WILSONART

Modern European-style cabinets, *contemporary track lighting and smooth marble countertops create a contemporary background for this eclectic kitchen. Unusual elements like the rough wood styling of the bar stools adds an old-time country flavor to the overall eclectic effect.*

LIST OF CONTRIBUTORS

We'd like to thank the following companies for providing the photographs used in this book:

American Olean Tile Company
1000 Cannon Avenue
Lansdale, PA 19446-0271
215-855-1111

The Amtico Company Limited
6480 Roswell Road
Atlanta, GA 30328
1-800-268-4260

Andersen Window Corporation
Bayport, MN 55003
1-800-654-3008

Armstrong World Industries Inc.
P.O. Box 8022
Plymouth, MI 48170-9948
1-800-704-8000

Crystal Cabinet Works, Inc.
1100 Crystal Drive
Princeton, MN 55371
612-389-4187

Bruce Hardwood Floors
A Division of Triangle Pacific Corp.
16803 Dallas Parkway
Dallas, TX 75428
800-526-0308

Color Tile Inc.
515 Houston Street
Fort Worth, TX 76102
Over 800 Color Tile & Carpet locations coast to coast.
For the store nearest you, call 1-800-NEARBY YOU

Congoleum Corporation
3705 Quackerbridge Road - Suite 211
P.O. Box 3127
Mercerville, NJ 08619-0127
609-584-3000

Dura Supreme
300 Dura Drive
Howard Lake, MN 55349
612-543-3872

Florida Tile Industries Inc.
P.O. Box 3900
Peoria, IL 61612
1-800-FLA-TILE

Kitchens & Baths by Lynn
Lynn Wallace, CKD
44489 Town Center Way, Suite. D254
Palm Desert, CA 92260
1-800-556-LYNN

Kitchens & Baths by Design;
David Skomsvold, designer
5276A Scotts Valley Drive
Scotts Valley, CA 95066
408-438-1843

KitchenAid Inc.
Whirlpool Corporation
Consumer Services
2303 Pipestone Road
Benton Harbor, MI 49022-2400

Karen Lehmann, ASID, CKD
Partners 4 Design
275 Market Street
Suite 109
Minneapolis, MN 55405
612-927-4444

Mannington Mills Inc.
P.O. Box 30
Salem, NJ 08079-0030
609-935-3000

Merillat Industries, Inc.
P.O. Box 1946
Adrian, MI 49221
517-263-0771

National Kitchen & Bath Association
687 Willow Grove Street
Hackettstown, NJ 07840
1-800-THE-NKBA

Quaker Maid,
A Division of WCI, Inc.
Route 61
Leesport, PA 19533
215-926-3011

WILSONART/Ralph Wilson Plastics Company
600 South General Bruce Drive
Temple, TX 75248
214-931-3000

Wood-Mode Inc.
No. 1, 2nd Street
Kreamer, PA 17833
717-374-2711